Original Title: 101 STRANGE BUT TRUE GOLF
FACTS

©101 STRANGE BUT TRUE GOLF FACTS,
Carlos Martínez Cerdá and Víctor Martínez
Cerdá, 2023

Authors: Víctor Martínez Cerdá and Carlos
Martínez Cerdá (V&C Brothers)

© Cover and illustrations: V&C Brothers

Layout and design: V&C Brothers

# 101
# STRANGE BUT TRUE
# GOLF FACTS

## AMAZING AND SURPRISING FACTS

# 1

**Golf courses are composed of a series of holes, each of which consists of a tee box, a fairway, and a putting green.**

Golf courses typically have a minimum of 9 holes, but ideally, they have 18 holes.

18-hole golf courses are divided into two sets of 9 holes, allowing players to stop after the first set if they wish.

The tee box is the starting point where the golf ball is placed to begin the stroke.

It is an elevated surface, usually made of grass, from which the player must hit the ball towards the fairway.

The fairway is the area that connects the tee box to the green.

It is a short and even grassy area that extends from the tee box to the putting green.

The fairway is surrounded by natural and artificial obstacles, such as trees, bushes, bunkers, lakes, and others.

The putting green is the area where the hole is located.

It is a very short and even grassy surface located at the end of the fairway.

The putting green is where the hole is completed, meaning that the player must putt the ball into the hole with the fewest strokes possible.

In addition to the holes, golf courses also typically have other areas such as bunkers, lakes, rough areas (long and difficult grass), among others.

These obstacles make the game more challenging and require more skill from the player.

# 2

**The International Golf Club of Massachusetts, located in Bolton, Massachusetts, United States, is home to the largest golf green in the world on its fifth hole.**

This green is known as the "Monster Green" due to its size and complexity.

The "Monster Green" has a total surface area of 28,000 square feet, which is approximately 2,600 square meters.

That is, it is larger than many soccer fields and can accommodate several golf flags.

The design of the "Monster Green" was created by golf course architect, Gil Hanse, and is characterized by its large size and oval shape.

Additionally, the green has several elevated sections and depressions, making it very challenging for players.

The fifth hole of the International Golf Club of Massachusetts is a par-5 that has a total length of 622 yards (approximately 568 meters).

It is one of the longest holes on the course and requires several shots to reach the green.

The "Monster Green" is a popular destination for golfers and attracts many tourists who want to see and play on the largest green in the world.

The International Golf Club of Massachusetts is a prestigious venue and has hosted several major golf tournaments over the years.

# 3

**Golf is a sport that requires skill, precision, and patience.**

One of the most exciting moments in golf is when a player makes a hole-in-one, which is when the ball goes directly into the hole from the tee with a single stroke.

The probability of an average golfer making a hole-in-one on any given hole is about 1 in 12,500.

However, this probability varies depending on the player's skill level and the conditions of the golf course.

It's important to note that making a hole-in-one is not an easy task and requires a lot of luck in addition to skill.

Some players can spend their entire lives playing golf without making a hole-in-one.

Furthermore, the chances of making two holes-in-one in a single round of golf are extremely low, with a probability of 1 in 67 million.

This is because making a hole-in-one is a rare and random event that depends on many factors, such as the distance of the hole, the conditions of the course, the wind, and the player's skill.

Despite the low odds, holes-in-one are an exciting moment for golfers and can be a great source of pride and satisfaction.

Many golf courses have a registry book where golfers can record their holes-in-one, which helps create a sense of community and celebrate the achievements of players.

# 4

**A regulation golf ball has 336 dimples on its surface, and this is an important characteristic that allows the ball to fly and stay in the air with a consistent trajectory.**

The dimples on the surface of the golf ball create a phenomenon called the "Magnus effect".

This means that as the ball moves through the air, the dimples create a turbulent airflow around the ball, which helps to reduce air resistance and increase the lift of the ball.

In addition, the dimples on the surface of the golf ball also help to create a "grip effect" on the ball.

When the ball impacts with the ground or a hard surface, the dimples help to create a grip effect that allows the ball to stop and stay in place.

It is important to note that the dimples on the surface of the golf ball are regulated by golf organizations such as the USGA (United States Golf Association) and the R&A (Royal and Ancient Golf Club of St Andrews).

These organizations have specific rules and regulations regarding the size, shape, and depth of the dimples on golf balls, to ensure the integrity and fairness of the game.

Overall, the dimples on the surface of the golf ball are an important feature that helps players achieve more accurate and consistent shots.

They are a fundamental part of the design of the golf ball and have been the subject of much research and testing to improve their effectiveness in the game.

# 5

**The golf bag is the basic equipment used by a golf player during a match.**

Usually, a golf bag is composed of 14 clubs, although some professional players may carry fewer.

It usually consists of four woods and ten irons.

Woods, also known as "drivers," are used for longer shots, such as shots from the tee or to reach the green in a few strokes.

Irons, on the other hand, are used for more precise shots, such as approach shots to the greens.

The putter is the most specialized club and is used to roll the ball on the green and into the hole.

Woods have large, rounded heads, which provide a large impact surface, and a long shaft, which gives them greater reach on the stroke.

Irons, on the other hand, have smaller heads and a greater amount of weight in the lower part of the head, which gives them greater precision in the stroke.

Irons are usually numbered from 1 to 9, with the 1-iron having the lowest loft angle and the 9-iron having the highest.

The higher the number of the iron club, the higher the loft angle, which means the ball will fly higher and have a shorter distance.

In addition to the irons from 1 to 9, there are also iron clubs known as wedges, which are used for special shots such as bunker shots or approach shots from short distances.

The putter, on the other hand, is the shortest club in the bag and has a flat, rectangular head that is used to roll the ball on the green and into the hole.

# 6

**Golf has traditionally been a sport dominated by men, but in recent decades there has been a growing interest and participation by women in golf.**

According to data from the United States Golf Association, in 2020, 24% of golfers in the United States were women.

In addition, the number of women playing golf has been increasing worldwide.

The first official women's golf tournament was held in Musselburgh, Scotland on January 1, 1881.

It was organized by the Edinburgh Ladies' Golf Club and featured seven players.

The tournament was played on the Musselburgh Links course, which had been used for golf since the 17th century.

Since then, women's golf has evolved considerably and several important tours and tournaments have been created for women, such as the LPGA Tour in the United States and the Ladies European Tour in Europe.

Women's golf has also been included in the Summer Olympics since 2016, with the women's golf tournament held in Rio de Janeiro, Brazil.

The Olympic women's golf tournament is played over 72 holes and features the participation of 60 golfers from around the world.

# 7

**The British Open, also known as The Open Championship, is the oldest golf tournament in the world.**

It was founded in 1860 and has been held annually since then, with the exception of the years during the two world wars.

The tournament is organized by The R&A (formerly known as The Royal and Ancient Golf Club of St Andrews), a golf organization based in Scotland.

The British Open is played on different golf courses in the United Kingdom, and is one of the four major golf tournaments (along with the Masters in Augusta, the US Open, and the PGA Championship).

The first winner of the British Open was Willie Park Sr., who won a prize of 12 British pounds.

Over the years, the tournament has been won by some of the best golfers in history, including Harry Vardon, Bobby Jones, Jack Nicklaus, Gary Player, Seve Ballesteros, Tiger Woods, and Rory McIlroy, among others.

In 2022, the 150th edition of the British Open was held at the St Andrews golf course in Scotland.

The winner of the tournament was Australian Daniel Popovic, who achieved his first victory in a major golf tournament.

# 8

**The Tactu Golf Club is a golf course located in the city of La Oroya, in the department of Junín, Peru.**

It is known for having the highest elevation of any golf course in the world, with an altitude of 4,369 meters above sea level.

This extreme altitude means that the air density is much lower than at golf courses located at lower altitudes, which affects the way the game is played.

Because the air density is lower, the golf ball travels further in the air at the Tactu Golf Club.

On average, golf balls can travel up to 20% more distance compared to the distance they would travel at a golf course at sea level.

This effect is due to the ball experiencing less air resistance and being able to maintain its speed for a longer time in the air.

Despite this advantage, playing golf at the Tactu Golf Club presents unique challenges.

The extreme altitude can affect the way the game is played and may require adjustments in technique and strategy.

The lack of oxygen in the air can also affect golfers' endurance and concentration.

In summary, the Tactu Golf Club in Peru is the golf course with the highest terrain in the world and the extreme altitude has a significant impact on the way the game is played, including the golf ball's ability to travel further in the air.

# 9

**The TPC at Sawgrass is a golf course located in Ponte Vedra Beach, Florida, United States.**

The course is known for its 17th hole, an island par 3 surrounded by water, which is considered one of the most iconic holes in golf.

Every year, around 125,000 golf balls are hit into the water on the 17th hole of the TPC at Sawgrass.

The 17th hole at TPC at Sawgrass is a 137-yard par 3 that requires a precise shot over the water to a small island on the green.

The island is surrounded by water in all directions, making it a very challenging hole for golfers.

The hole is famous for the fact that professional golfers playing in the annual PGA Tour tournament, The Players Championship, often struggle to get a good result on this hole.

The fact that so many golf balls are hit into the water on the 17th hole at TPC at Sawgrass is largely due to the difficulty of the hole and the number of golfers who attempt to play it throughout the year.

Many of the golfers playing on the course are tourists and amateurs, which means they don't have the skill and experience necessary to make a good shot on this particular hole.

In addition, the 17th hole at TPC at Sawgrass also attracts many spectators during The Players Championship tournament, which means there are more people watching the shots and therefore increases the likelihood of golf balls ending up in the water.

In conclusion, the 17th hole at TPC at Sawgrass is an iconic island par 3 that is located on a golf course in Florida, United States.

Due to its difficulty and popularity, around 125,000 golf balls are hit into the water on the 17th hole every year.

# 10

**Golf is a sport that focuses on the reach and precision of the stroke, which leads to records being set for the longest distances that can be achieved in a single stroke.**

In this sense, two particular records have been recorded, which are the longest drive in history and the longest putt in history.

The longest drive in history ever recorded is 470 meters, which is truly impressive.

This record is attributed to Mike Austin, an American golfer who achieved this stroke in the Senior World Championship in 1974.

This record has been the subject of controversy, as some golfers have claimed to have surpassed this mark, but have not been officially recorded.

On the other hand, the longest putt in history is a monstrous 114 meters.

This record has also been subject to debate, as some golfers have claimed to have made even longer putts, but without official registration.

The longest recorded putt was made by Fergus Muir in the Greenore Open Tournament in 2001.

It is important to note that these records are extremely rare and not representative of the typical strokes of an average golfer.

Most golfers can hit their drive an average distance of around 220 to 280 meters, while most typical putts are less than 5 meters.

Therefore, these records are exceptions and not the norm in the world of golf.

# 11

**Phil Mickelson, also known as "Lefty", is a professional American golfer who is famous for playing golf with a left-handed swing, despite being right-handed.**

Mickelson learned to play golf from his father, who was also right-handed, but decided to mimic his swing in reverse in the mirror, which allowed him to effectively play as a lefty.

Since then, Mickelson has used left-handed golf clubs in his professional career and has achieved great success in golf, including 5 wins in PGA Tour Major tournaments.

His left-handed playing style has also made him unique in the world of golf, as it is rare to see a right-handed golfer play with a left-handed swing.

The fact that Mickelson is right-handed but plays as a lefty is itself a testament to his skill and adaptability as a golfer.

Despite his playing style putting him at a disadvantage in some situations, Mickelson has demonstrated great skill and versatility in his career, which has made him one of the most successful and recognized golfers in the world.

In summary, Phil Mickelson is a professional right-handed golfer who learned to play golf by mimicking his father's golf swing in reverse in the mirror.

Since then, he has used left-handed golf clubs in his professional career and achieved great success in golf.

His left-handed playing style makes him unique in the world of golf and is a testament to his skill and adaptability as a golfer.

# 12

**Golf balls fly much farther on hot days due to the physics of how temperature affects air density.**

As temperature increases, air expands and becomes less dense, meaning there is less air resistance for a golf ball in flight.

As a result, the golf ball can travel farther.

More specifically, it has been shown that for every 4 degrees Celsius the temperature increases, a golfer swinging a club at around 140 km/h can carry the driver up to 5 meters farther.

This may seem like a small amount, but in the world of golf, where every meter counts, it can make a big difference in the distance that can be covered in a single shot.

It is important to note that temperature is not the only factor that affects the distance of the golf ball.

Other factors such as humidity, altitude, barometric pressure, and the strength and direction of the wind can also have a significant impact on the distance of the golf ball in flight.

# 13

**The International Golf Club in Bolton, Massachusetts, is a private and exclusive golf course that opened its doors in 2001.**

The golf course features 18 holes and has been designed by the famous golf course architect, Tom Fazio.

In addition to being the longest golf course in the world at 7,612 meters, it is also considered one of the most difficult.

The course par is 77, which means the golfer must complete the course in a total of 77 strokes or less.

With a total of five par 5s and five par 3s, the course has eight par 4s, making it extremely challenging to complete in par.

The fifth hole of the International Golf Club in Massachusetts is the largest golf green in the world.

With an area of over 28,000 square feet, this par 6 is known as "The Himalayas" due to the enormous elevation that must be overcome to reach the green.

The hole measures 644 yards from the tee box and requires at least six strokes to reach the green.

# 14

**The 7th hole at Satsuki Golf Club in Sano, Japan is known as the longest golf hole in the world.**

This par 7 hole is a unique challenge for golfers looking to test their skills on the course.

The hole measures approximately 831 meters from the tee to the green, which means that players must travel more than 900 yards to complete it.

Satsuki Golf Club is a private golf course located in the Sano prefecture in the Kanto region of Japan.

The course was designed by golf architect Kinya Fujita in 1972 and has remained one of the most popular and respected courses in Japan ever since.

The 7th hole at Satsuki is known for its extreme length, which means that players must have great power and precision in their shots to successfully complete the hole.

The hole starts on an elevated tee and winds through a wooded landscape before arriving at a green surrounded by bunkers and a pond.

Although the 7th hole at Satsuki Golf Club is the longest golf hole in the world, it is not the longest on all golf courses.

The length of holes varies depending on the design and location of the course.

However, the 7th hole at Satsuki remains an impressive milestone in the history of golf and a true challenge for golfers around the world.

# 15

**The 7th hole of the Pine Valley Golf Club in New Jersey, USA, features one of the largest bunkers in the world.**

This gigantic bunker is known as "Hell's Half Acre" and is one of the biggest challenges for golfers who play at Pine Valley.

Pine Valley Golf Club is one of the most exclusive and prestigious golf courses in the world, and is considered by many to be the best golf course in the United States.

It was designed by George Crump and Harry Colt in 1913, and has since undergone many renovations and improvements.

The 7th hole is a par 5 and is considered one of the most difficult holes on the course.

Hell's Half Acre is a crescent-shaped bunker that extends along the left side of the fairway and surrounds the green.

This bunker measures approximately 23,000 square feet, making it one of the largest bunkers in the world.

Hell's Half Acre bunker presents a great challenge for golfers, as it requires a precise and strategic shot to avoid getting trapped in it.

If a player ends up in the bunker, it can be difficult to get out of it and reach the green in the next shot.

The design of Pine Valley Golf Club is known for its natural beauty and technical demand, and Hell's Half Acre is an example of the creativity and challenge that Crump and Colt incorporated into their design.

Although only club members have access to the course, Pine Valley is one of the most famous and admired golf courses in the world for its innovative and challenging design, as well as the exclusivity of its memberships.

# 16

**The average swing speed of a female golfer's driver is 99 km/h.**

-154 km/h for an average LPGA professional.

-135 km/h for an average male golfer.

-173 km/h for an average PGA Tour player.

-210 km/h for Tiger Woods.

-240 km/h for a long drive champion.

# 17

**The first golf balls date back to the 15th century and were made of leather stuffed with bird feathers.**

These balls were very soft and not very durable, so they deformed easily during play and could not be used for very long.

Over time, different materials were experimented with to improve the durability and quality of golf balls.

In the 1840s, gutta-percha balls began to be manufactured, a substance obtained from the resin of certain tropical trees.

These balls were more durable and could be molded more easily, allowing for a more spherical shape.

Despite these improvements, gutta-percha balls still had a problem: their smooth surface meant they had limited reach in the air, affecting golfers' play.

This was because being smooth, they offered more air resistance than dimpled balls.

It was in 1905 when it was discovered that dimpled balls could fly farther and with greater accuracy than smooth balls.

The dimple design allowed air to flow more efficiently around the ball, reducing resistance and increasing ball speed and distance.

Since then, constant improvements have been made in the materials and designs of golf balls, with the aim of optimizing their performance and improving the playing experience for golfers.

Today's modern golf balls are made of materials such as urethane or ionomer and have advanced dimple designs that allow for a straighter flight and greater distance in the air.

# 18

**Coby Orr is known for being the youngest golfer in history to make a hole in one.**

He was born in 1970 and grew up in Littleton, Colorado, where he began playing golf at a young age.

In 1975, when he was five years old, Coby Orr was playing at the Eagle Trace golf course in Littleton with his father and older brother.

On the 11th hole, a par 3 of 81 yards, Coby took his golf club and made his shot.

The ball landed on the green and rolled straight towards the hole, without needing any bounce, before dropping into it.

Coby, his father, and his brother erupted in shouts of joy and surprise at the incredible shot by the child.

The feat quickly spread through the media, and Coby became a national sensation.

He received a great deal of media attention and was invited to appear on several television programs, including Johnny Carson's "The Tonight Show."

Despite his achievement, Coby Orr did not become a professional golfer.

After growing up, he became an entrepreneur and continued to play golf as an amateur.

However, his name will always be remembered in the history of golf as the youngest player to make a hole in one.

# 19

**The world's longest golf hole is located at the Gunsan Country Club in South Korea, on its 3rd hole.**

This hole is known as the "par 7" and has a length of 1 km (1,098 yards), making it one of the longest holes in the world.

The hole itself is a stunning landscape and is surrounded by the mountains of North Jeolla Province.

Golfers need to make a series of precise shots to reach the green and then make a successful putt to finish the hole.

It is important to note that this hole is extremely difficult and only the most skilled and experienced players have any chance of completing it in a reasonable number of strokes.

Most golfers need several shots just to reach the middle of the fairway, and some have even reported needing more than 20 shots to finish the hole.

Despite its difficulty, this hole is a great attraction for many golfers who want to test their luck and face the challenge of the world's longest hole.

# 20

**There is a widespread rumor on the internet that claims that "golf" is an acronym that stands for "Gentlemen Only Women Forbidden".**

However, according to the United States Golf Association (USGA), "golf" comes from "kolf" or "kolve", which meant "club" in medieval Dutch.

Although it is worth noting that women were excluded from the sport until the 18th century, when the first women's match was played in Musselburgh, Scotland.

# 21

**Chuiwan is a traditional Chinese sport that bears
many similarities to modern golf.**

It is believed to have originated during the Tang dynasty in the 8th
century, although it became popular during the
Song dynasty in the 11th century.

The goal of the game is to put a ball into a hole in the ground,
using different clubs to strike the ball.

Like in golf, the objective is to do so in the fewest
number of strokes possible.

Chuiwan was originally played in large gardens and parks, where
playing fields with obstacles and holes were built.

Players used a variety of clubs of different lengths and shapes
to make different types of shots.

The sport was very popular among the aristocrats and high
society in China during the Song dynasty.

Chuiwan is often considered a possible source
of inspiration for modern golf.

Many sports historians believe that Scottish missionaries and
traders who visited China in the 19th century became familiar
with the game and brought it back to Europe.

In fact, the term "golf" is believed to come from the Dutch word
"kolf," which means stick or club, and may have been
used to describe Chuiwan.

In any case, Chuiwan remains a popular sport in China and is still
played today, especially in the Beijing region.

There are even annual Chuiwan competitions and tournaments
held throughout China.

# 22

**A hole in one is an impressive achievement in golf, which involves making a shot with a single ball from the tee to the hole in one play.**

It is a major milestone for any golfer, but making a longer hole in one is even more impressive.

The world record for the longest hole in one is held by Lou Kretlow, a professional golfer and former professional basketball player.

In 1961, on the Lowry Air Force Base golf course in Denver, Colorado, Kretlow made a hole in one that traveled 427 yards (390 meters) on the par-4 5th hole.

It is important to note that this was a par-4 hole, meaning that Kretlow had to make the shot on his first stroke from the tee to achieve the hole in one.

Kretlow's shot was a perfect tee shot, which soared through the air and flew over 390 meters before landing directly in the hole.

The feat was recognized as the longest hole in one in the history of golf and has remained the world record since then.

Although Kretlow's record remains impressive, there have been other attempts to break it.

In 1971, Mike Austin made a hole in one of 400 yards (366 meters) in a tournament at Green Valley Ranch golf course in Colorado, but the shot was made on a par-5 hole, which technically does not count as a hole in one.

In summary, the world record for the longest hole in one is 390 meters and was achieved by Lou Kretlow on a par-4 hole in 1961.

It is an impressive feat and remains one of the most notable in the history of golf.

# 23

**Golf is the only sport that has been played on the lunar surface so far.**

On February 6th, 1971, astronaut Alan Shepard, commander of NASA's Apollo 14 mission, took advantage of the moon's low gravity to play an impromptu game of golf.

Shepard, who was also the first American astronaut in space, brought a golf club and two golf balls with him on his trip to the moon.

After successfully completing the mission's tasks, Shepard decided to take a break and play a round of golf on the lunar surface.

With the help of astronaut Edgar Mitchell, who helped prepare the "green" on the lunar surface, Shepard used a 6-iron to make his shot.

His first golf ball failed in its attempt, as it veered off course, but his second attempt was a success.

Shepard reported that the ball traveled about 200 yards before landing on the lunar surface.

Shepard described his feat as "one small swing for a man, but one giant leap for mankind," making a play on words with Neil Armstrong's famous phrase when he first stepped on the moon.

Although the golf game on the moon was a fun and curious moment, it also had a scientific purpose.

Shepard wanted to demonstrate how the golf ball would behave in the moon's low gravity and how its flight would be different from what is experienced on Earth.

Scientists also used the opportunity to measure the force and distance of the shots.

# 24

**In 1457, the king of Scotland, James II, issued a decree prohibiting the practice and matches of golf throughout Scottish territory.**

The reason behind this measure is not entirely clear, but it is believed to have been due to concerns about safety and national defense.

At that time, golf was a very popular sport in Scotland and was played in open fields and public places, which may have been seen as a distraction for young people and the population in general.

In addition, the ban may have been a measure to ensure that men were better prepared for the impending invasion of England.

This prohibition was reiterated in 1471, when King James III issued an edict again prohibiting golf.

Reportedly, the legend of Scottish golf, the famous golfer King James IV, ignored this prohibition and continued playing golf during his reign.

Despite these prohibitions, golf continued to be popular in Scotland, and in the 16th century, some of the oldest golf courses in the world were opened.

Over time, golf became an international sport and a popular pastime all over the world, including Scotland, where the British Open is held annually, one of the four most important golf tournaments in the world.

# 25

**The oldest golf course in the world is Musselburgh Links in Scotland, which is located about 6 kilometers east of Edinburgh.**

The course is situated on flat land, located alongside the estuary of the River Esk, and is believed to have been used for playing golf since the 17th century.

There is documentary evidence supporting the claim that golf was played at Musselburgh Links since 1672, making it one of the oldest golf courses in the world.

In addition, there are records that the course was designed by the famous golf course designer, Old Tom Morris, in 1870.

However, some golf historians claim that the game was played at Musselburgh Links much earlier, and that Queen Mary I of Scotland played golf there around 1567.

It is also said that this queen was the first woman to play golf, although there is no conclusive evidence to support this claim.

In any case, Musselburgh Links is a historic site for golf and has remained in use for centuries.

The course is notable for its flat terrain and coastal landscape, and it remains one of the most popular golf courses in Scotland and worldwide.

# 26

**The origin of the "birdie". The concept of a "birdie" refers to scoring one under par.**

But this term is relatively young in the sport, its origin dates back to a day in 1899 at the Atlantic City Country Club Northfield (in New Jersey, USA).

In a match between a small group of three golfers (George Crump, William Poultney Smith and his brother Ab Smith), one of them, on his second shot on a par 4 hole, hit a bird that was flying over the course, and the ball landed a few inches from the hole on the green.

The golfers called what happened a "birdie" and the word quickly caught on at their club to refer to shots that end up one stroke under the hole's par.

Over time, the concept spread throughout the United States and ended up being used by golfers all over the world.

Additionally, other terms emerged from it, such as eagle (scoring 2 strokes under par), albatross (3 under), and condor (4 under).

# 27

**The size of the holes is a fundamental part of the game of golf.**

The holes are the targets where players must hit the ball with the fewest number of strokes possible.

The current size of the golf holes is 4.25 inches (108 mm) in diameter, which means that the circle around the hole has this measurement.

Additionally, the hole must be at least 4 inches (100 mm) deep.

This standard measurement is due to a decision made by the officials of the Musselburgh Links in Scotland in the 19th century.

They chose a diameter that fit the size of a drainage pipe they had available at that time.

This measurement soon became standardized on all golf courses around the world and became the official size for golf holes.

It is interesting to note that throughout the history of golf, the size of the holes has varied.

In the early days of golf, the holes were much larger, often with a diameter of up to 8 inches (200 mm) or more.

Over time, the size was gradually reduced to the current standard of 4.25 inches.

In addition to the size, the positioning of the hole on the green is also an important factor in the game of golf.

Golfers must take into account the location of the hole and the way the green is sloped to decide how to make the shot and achieve the best possible outcome.

# 28

**In times of heat, environmental conditions can significantly affect the game of golf.**

Here are some important aspects to consider:

- **Temperature:** As the temperature increases, the golf ball expands slightly, which can affect how the ball reacts in the air and on the ground. Additionally, players may experience fatigue and dehydration if they don't hydrate adequately during the game.

- **Humidity:** In high humidity conditions, the air is denser, which can affect the distance the ball travels. Humidity can also affect the grip of the golf ball on the golf club, which can affect the player's control over the ball.

- **Altitude:** Altitude can affect the distance of the golf ball due to the decrease in air density as one goes higher in altitude. This means that in higher altitude places, the ball can travel farther.

- **Wind:** Wind is one of the most important factors in the game of golf, as it can significantly affect the trajectory and distance the ball travels.

In general, in times of heat, the golf ball tends to travel farther because the air is less dense.

This means that golfers can adjust their shots and use this advantage to their favor.

However, it is important to consider other factors such as humidity and wind, as well as staying hydrated during the game.

# 29

**Tees are small pieces of wood, plastic, or similar material that are used to elevate the golf ball off the ground on the first stroke of each hole.**

The tees are placed on the ground and the ball is placed on top of the tee, allowing the player to make a clean and effective swing.

Before the invention of golf tees, golf players had to build small mounds of sand or earth to support the ball on the first stroke.

These mounds were called "teeing grounds" and were often in poor condition, making the game more difficult.

The invention of the modern tee is credited to a golf player named William Bloxsom in 1899, who designed a small wooden support to hold the ball on the first stroke.

Since then, tees have become an essential part of the game of golf.

Tees come in different sizes and materials, and can vary in height and shape according to the player's preferences and the conditions of the golf course.

# 30

**Caddies are the ones who carry the bag with the clubs and advise the golfer.**

Formerly, this sport was only for royalty and aristocrats, so they were always accompanied by someone who carried their playing equipment.

In the 1560s, Queen of Scotland, Mary Stuart, returned from France, where she fell in love with golf.

She was the one who introduced the French term Cadet, which was given to the person who carried her clubs.

The choice of this term is due to the fact that in her country, military cadets were assigned to unimportant tasks.

# 31

**Golf clubs have evolved throughout history and have undergone numerous changes in their design and manufacturing materials.**

In the origins of golf, dating back to the 15th century in Scotland, clubs were very different from those used today.

At that time, golf clubs were handmade by local craftsmen and were mainly made of ash and hazelwood.

The use of these materials was because they were easy to find in the areas near golf courses and were strong enough to withstand the impact of the golf ball without breaking.

However, these clubs were quite heavy and did not allow for the same precision and distance as modern clubs.

Over time, other materials such as iron and steel were incorporated into the manufacturing of golf clubs.

This allowed clubs to be lighter and stronger, which in turn improved the accuracy and distance of shots.

Today, golf clubs are made with advanced materials such as graphite and titanium, which allow for greater flexibility and precision in shots.

In addition, club designs have evolved to adapt to the different needs of golfers according to their level of play and personal preferences.

# 32

**Golf is a sport in which the goal is to hit a ball with a club towards a hole in the fewest possible number of strokes.**

The player who completes the course in the fewest number of strokes wins the tournament.

Unlike other sports where the goal is to score the most points, golf is the only professional scoring sport where the player with the lowest score wins.

That is, the player who completes the course in fewer strokes is the winner.

The scoring system in golf is based on the number of strokes the player needs to complete each hole on the golf course.

Generally, golf courses have 18 holes, so the final result is obtained by adding up the total number of strokes the player needed to complete all 18 holes.

In addition, golf also uses a score relative to the course par.

The course par refers to the number of strokes that an average skilled player is expected to need to complete each hole.

If a player completes a hole in fewer strokes than the course par, they receive a negative score.

On the other hand, if they need more strokes than the course par, they receive a positive score.

# 33

**Golf was considered a relatively recent Olympic sport, as its return to the Olympic Games occurred in Rio de Janeiro in 2016 after an absence of over 100 years.**

Golf had been an Olympic sport in the early editions of the modern Olympic Games, in Paris 1900 and St. Louis 1904.

However, it was excluded from later Games due to several reasons, such as lack of interest and absence of international stars.

For many years, efforts to reintroduce golf to the Olympic Games were unsuccessful, but it was finally accepted again as an Olympic sport at the 121st session of the International Olympic Committee in Copenhagen in 2009.

The decision was made with the intention of attracting a younger audience and expanding the sport's base.

At the Rio 2016 Olympic Games, individual men's and women's competitions were held, and players were ranked according to the world golf rankings.

Golf was also included in the Tokyo 2020 Olympic Games, which were held in 2021 due to the COVID-19 pandemic.

# 34

**Americans spend a significant amount of money
every year on golf balls.**

According to the U.S. Golf Industry Association, it is estimated
that over $600 million was spent on golf balls
in the United States in 2020.

The golf ball is a crucial item in this sport and is one of the most
important consumables that a player needs to play golf.

Golf balls can vary in price, from the most affordable to high-end
ones, which can cost several dollars per unit.

As for the first televised golf championship, it is true that
it was played in Chicago in 1953.

It was the 1953 U.S. Open Championship, one of the four major
professional men's golf tournaments.

This was the first time a golf event was
broadcast live on television.

The television coverage was limited and only aired in a few cities
in the U.S., but it laid the foundation for the growing popularity
of golf on television in the decades that followed.

Since then, golf has been one of the most popular sports on
television and has been broadcast around the world, including
major events such as the Masters, the British Open, the U.S.
Open, and the PGA Championship.

Television has been a key factor in popularizing golf, leading to
increased participation and interest in the sport worldwide.

# 35

**Tiger Woods, one of the most successful golfers in history, suffers from allergies to grass and some trees that are found on golf courses.**

This allergy can cause symptoms such as itchy eyes, sneezing, and breathing problems, which can affect his performance on the course.

To treat this allergy and improve his vision, Woods underwent laser eye surgery in 1999 when he was 23 years old.

The surgery, known as LASIK, is a procedure in which a laser is used to reshape the cornea of the eye, which can improve vision and reduce the need for glasses or contact lenses.

After the surgery, Woods said that his vision had significantly improved and that he could see sharper details on the course, which improved his game.

Since then, he has been an advocate for laser eye surgery and has encouraged other athletes to consider it if they have vision problems.

Despite the eye surgery, Woods still suffers from allergies and has had to take measures to avoid symptoms during his tournaments.

For example, in the past, he has worn protective glasses to prevent grass particles from entering his eyes and has taken antiallergic medication to control symptoms.

# 36

**William Ruggles MacKenzie.**

Born on September 28, 1974 in Greenville, North Carolina, he is an American professional golfer who has played on the PGA Tour.

After a semester at Lees-McRae College, Will took the money he earned washing dishes and selling grilled cheese sandwiches at Grateful Dead concerts and moved out west.

After some time working for Taco Bell in Jackson Hole, Wyoming, he spent the next five winters snowboarding while living in a van in Big Sky, Montana.

At one point, he spent 30 days living in a snow cave near Valdez, Alaska, without showering, and snowboarding in the Chugach Mountains before ending up frostbitten.

During the warmer months, he rock climbed and became a Class V kayaker before working as a rafting guide in Montana and its Gallatin River, West Virginia and its Gauley River, and rivers around North Carolina.

He returned to Greenville, North Carolina in 1999, earning enough money selling Christmas trees to embark on a three-month surf trip to Costa Rica.

Unfortunately, when he returned home and tried to make a living selling hammocks, he ended up deeply in debt.

However, a glimpse on television of his childhood idol, Payne Stewart, winning the 1999 US Open reignited his love for the game and he decided to play professionally.

He turned pro in 2000 and in 2013, MacKenzie played the entire season on the Web.com Tour, finishing 40th on the money list and regaining his PGA Tour privileges through the Web.com Tour Finals.

On the PGA Tour in 2014, he finished second in the Valero Texas Open and fourth in the Valspar Championship.

# 37

**The Ice Golf World Championship, also known as the Arctic Open, is an annual event held in Uummannaq, a small town on the west coast of Greenland.**

The tournament was founded in 1999 by a group of local golfers who wanted to find a way to enjoy their favorite sport in a winter environment.

The tournament takes place on the sea ice surrounding the city of Uummannaq, with temperatures dropping as low as -50 Celsius.

The championship lasts for 2 days and has 36 holes hand-sculpted in the snow and ice, and they can vary in length and difficulty.

Players use normal golf balls, but the clubs are made of special materials that can withstand the extremely cold temperatures.

The tournament is unique for its location and weather conditions, and the 36 players face unique challenges such as the lack of grass and the fact that the ball can bounce unpredictably on the hard and slippery surface.

They also have to deal with extreme cold and lack of sunlight, as at this time of year, the sun doesn't rise for several weeks.

The event has attracted players from around the world and has gained popularity in recent years, thanks in part to the growing attention to climate change and its impact on Arctic regions.

In addition to the tournament itself, there are a series of social and cultural events that take place in Uummannaq during the Arctic Open, including dinners, live music, and sled excursions.

# 38

**Nick Faldo is a British golfer who has achieved
great feats in his career.**

He was born on July 18, 1957 in England and started
playing golf from a young age.

He won his first major tournament in 1987, when he claimed
the US Open at Muirfield Village Golf Club.

Throughout his career, Faldo won a total of six Grand Slam
tournaments, including three British Open championships and
three Masters championships at Augusta.

He was also ranked as the world number one for a total of 97
weeks and played on 11 European Ryder Cup teams,
where he served as captain in 2008.

In addition to his accomplishments on the golf course,
Nick Faldo has worked as a television commentator
and golf course designer.

In 2009, he was knighted by Queen Elizabeth II for his
services to golf and his charitable work through the Nick
Faldo Foundation, which promotes the development
of young golfers around the world.

As for the Faldo Course, it is a golf course designed by Nick
Faldo at the Lough Erne Resort in Northern Ireland.

It was opened in 2009 and has been awarded several awards
for its design and quality, including the award for Best New
Golf Course in Europe in 2010.

# 39

**The claim that 90% of Fortune 500 CEOs play golf is a commonly cited statistic, although there is no reliable source to support this specific claim.**

However, it is true that golf has long been a popular sport among executives and business leaders.

There are several reasons why golf is appealing to executives and business leaders.

Firstly, golf is a sport that can be played and enjoyed throughout a lifetime, which means many executives have been playing golf for many years and have developed skills and networks in the process.

Additionally, golf is a sport that lends itself to conversation and networking, making it an ideal activity for establishing informal business relationships.

Many people say that golf helps them create new business relationships and strengthen existing ones.

Finally, golf also lends itself to competition and challenge, which can appeal to results-oriented individuals who enjoy personal achievement.

The game also requires concentration and patience, which are valuable characteristics for business leaders.

# 40

**Golf is a popular and well-known sport worldwide, and it has a number of major tours.**

**Golf Tours:**

- **PGA Tour:** is the leading professional men's golf tour in the United States, and it is where many of the world's best golfers compete. The PGA Tour consists of a series of events held in different cities across the United States throughout the year.

- **Web.com Tour:** is another professional men's golf tour in the United States. It is considered the second level of the PGA Tour and serves as a pathway for players to qualify for the PGA Tour.

- **PGA Tour Latinoamérica:** is a professional men's golf tour held in various countries in Latin America. It is a platform for Latin American golfers to compete and develop before moving on to larger tours.

- **European Tour:** is the leading professional men's golf tour in Europe. The tour has a series of events held in different European countries throughout the year.

- **Asian Tour:** is the leading professional men's golf tour in Asia. The tour has a series of events held in different Asian countries throughout the year.

# 41

## Benefits of Playing Golf.

Did you know that playing a round of golf can lead you to walk up to 10 kilometers?

It may seem like a very passive sport, but it really isn't.

The golfer covers long distances between holes, albeit at a slower pace, but it is still a cardio exercise that you are doing.

In fact, it is estimated that a golfer burns 700 kilocalories during a 9-hole round.

And if you want to lose weight or avoid overweight, you can increase the speed and turn it into a more aerobic exercise.

Regular practice improves muscle flexibility, is gentle on the joints, and helps tone the abdomen, back, arms, and chest.

# 42

**The sport of golf has a long and rich history dating back several centuries.**

As for the first golfer, it's difficult to determine exactly who that was, as the sport evolved gradually over time and there's no specific moment when it can be said to have been played for the first time.

However, when it comes to the first professional golfers, Walter Hagen is widely considered to be one of the first golfers to make a living as a player rather than as a golf instructor.

Born in 1892 in New York, Hagen was one of the most successful golfers of his time, winning a total of 11 Grand Slam titles over the course of his career.

In addition to his achievements on the course, Hagen was also a pioneer in golf marketing and advertising.

He was one of the first golfers to charge commercial brands for advertising, and his popularity and charisma made him a highly influential figure in the world of golf.

In summary, while the first golfer in history cannot be determined, Walter Hagen was one of the first professional golfers and one of the most successful of his time, as well as a pioneer in golf marketing and advertising.

# 43

**Golf is a sport that moves a large amount of money worldwide.**

According to data from consulting firm KPMG, the direct economic impact of golf in Europe is over €12.7 billion and generates around 121,000 jobs.

One of the main economic drivers of golf are golf courses, which generate €777 million in direct revenues through the sale of green fees, membership fees, equipment rental, and other related services.

These direct revenues also translate into direct employment in the golf industry, such as golf course employees, golf instructors, industry professionals, and other related workers.

In addition, golf tourism is another important component of the economic impact of golf.

According to KPMG, golf tourists' spending in Europe amounts to around €4.64 billion, which represents a great opportunity for tourist destinations that offer golf courses and other golf-related services.

# 44

**The PGA Tour is the organization that governs professional golf in the United States and North America.**

Every year, it hosts a series of tournaments in which the world's best golfers compete for cash prizes and other honors.

The most prestigious tournament on the PGA Tour is the PGA Championship, one of the four most important golf tournaments in the world, known as "majors".

The winner of this tournament receives a cash prize of several million dollars, depending on the year.

In the 2021 edition of the PGA Championship, winner Phil Mickelson took home a cash prize of $2.16 million.

This amount is a fraction of the total prize money for the tournament, which was $12 million.

However, the PGA Tour also organizes the FedEx Cup playoffs competition, which is a series of three tournaments that take place after the PGA Championship.

The winner of the FedEx Cup final takes home a cash prize of $15 million, which is the largest individual monetary reward in golf.

Therefore, the winner of the FedEx Cup can receive a total of $18 million in cash prizes: $3 million for winning the first two playoffs tournaments and $15 million for winning the final.

In total, the FedEx Cup competition distributed a cash prize of $60 million in 2021, with an additional $15 million prize for players who finished second in the final standings.

# 45

**A caddie is the person who assists a golfer during a golf tournament or practice, carrying their clubs, advising on club selection, and providing information about the course conditions.**

The salary of a golf caddie in the United States can vary widely depending on several factors, such as experience, demand, location, and the skill level of the golfer they are assisting.

However, according to data from various sources, the average salary of a caddie in the United States ranges between $30,000 and $40,000 per year.

In the specific case of New York, according to information from the job platform Indeed, the average salary of a caddie is around $30,000 per month, which translates to about $360,000 per year.

In addition, caddies can receive tips from golfers that can add up to several thousand additional dollars per year.

It is important to note that a caddie's salary can also vary depending on the type of tournament or event the golfer is participating in.

In some cases, caddies can receive a portion of the golfer's cash prize if they win the tournament.

Overall, the job of a caddie can be a good option for those who enjoy golf and are looking for a flexible job, but it is important to keep in mind that demand can vary depending on the season and geographical location.

# 46

**Golf is a sport played on a course with 18 holes,
each with a determined par.**

The time it takes to play a round of golf depends on several
factors, such as the number of players, the skill level of the
players, and the pace of play on the course.

The United States Golf Association (USGA) has established
some guidelines for golf pace of play.

In general, the maximum time for a round of 18 holes should not
exceed the following recommendations:

**–For a group of 4 players:** 4 hours and 50 minutes.

**–For a group of 2 players:** 4 hours and 10 minutes.

However, it is important to note that these are
recommendations and not strict rules.

The actual time of play may vary depending on various factors,
such as congestion on the course, the number of players, the
skill level of the players, and weather and course conditions.

To help maintain pace of play, many golf courses have a course
marshal or supervisor who monitors the players' pace of play
and may ask them to move faster if they are behind.

In addition, players can also do their part to maintain a proper
pace of play, such as walking quickly, preparing for their shots
while others play, and limiting the time spent
searching for lost balls.

# 47

**The US Open is one of the four major golf tournaments (Grand Slam) and is organized by the United States Golf Association (USGA).**

It is known for being one of the most prestigious and difficult tournaments to win in the world of golf.

The cash prize for the winner of the US Open has significantly increased in recent years.

In the 2021 edition, the winner of the tournament received a cash prize of $2.6 million, which represents a 12.5% increase compared to the $2.25 million cash prize from the previous year.

The total cash prize for the 2021 US Open was $12.5 million, meaning the winner received approximately 21% of the total cash prize.

Additionally, players who finish in top positions also receive a portion of the cash prize, and the cash prize for runners-up is $1.3 million.

It is important to note that the cash prize for the US Open can vary from year to year and may also depend on the location where the tournament is held.

In general, major golf tournaments, such as the US Open, tend to have significantly larger cash prizes than other regular golf tournaments.

# 48

**The Players Championship is one of the most important tournaments in the PGA Tour calendar and is known for having one of the largest prize purses in professional golf.**

The 2022 edition of the tournament had a record prize purse of 20 million dollars, which represents a 33% increase from the 15 million dollar prize purse in 2021.

The winner of the 2022 Players Championship was Cameron Smith, who took home a cash prize of 3.6 million dollars for his victory in the tournament.

This was Smith's first win in the Players Championship and the biggest victory of his career on the PGA Tour.

Smith won the tournament after an exciting playoff against South African Christiaan Bezuidenhout.

The cash prize for the winner of the Players Championship represents approximately 18% of the total prize purse for the tournament.

Second place in the tournament, Christiaan Bezuidenhout, took home a cash prize of 1.35 million dollars, while the four players who tied for third place, including American Justin Thomas, each earned 563,333 dollars.

# 49

**Dressing appropriately to play golf is important both out of respect for the sport and for comfort on the course.**

Here are some general guidelines on how to dress for golf:

**–Shirts or polos:** It is recommended to wear short or long-sleeved shirts or polos with a collar. These garments should be specifically designed for golf and made of fabrics that allow good ventilation and sweat absorption. It is important that shirts are tucked into pants and buttons are fastened.

**–Pants:** Pants specifically designed for golf should be worn, which are usually made of cotton or cotton-polyester blends. Pants should be long and fitted, but not too tight. Shorts can be worn in warm weather, but they should be of appropriate length and never too short.

**–Shoes:** Golf shoes are necessary to provide adequate traction and stability on the course. Shoes should be comfortable and of good quality to avoid blisters and foot injuries.

**–Accessories:** It is recommended to wear a cap or visor to protect oneself from the sun and maintain good visibility on the course. Golf gloves are also important to provide a good grip on the club. It is also common to wear a lightweight jacket or vest in colder weather.

It is important to note that many golf courses have specific dress codes that must be followed.

For example, some courses may prohibit the use of shorts or require that pants be a specific color.

It is important to check with the course before playing to ensure compliance with their dress code.

# 50

**In golf, the number of strokes a professional player or golf handicap is expected to take to complete a hole or an entire course is called "par".**

The number of strokes expected for a golfer to complete a hole varies depending on the length and difficulty of the hole.

Most golf courses have a total par of 72 for 18 holes, but this can vary depending on the course design.

Holes are typically classified by their par, which can be 3, 4, or 5 strokes.

Par 3 holes are usually the shortest and easiest, while par 5 holes are the longest and most difficult.

Par 4 holes are of medium length and offer a balanced challenge for golfers.

The total number of strokes a player takes to complete a hole or an entire course is called "score".

A player wants to have a low score, which means they took fewer strokes to complete the course.

It's important to note that players can take more or fewer strokes than par on each hole, and this will affect their total score.

If a player takes fewer strokes than par on a hole, it's called a "birdie".

If they take more strokes than par, it's called a "bogey".

If they take two strokes more than par, it's called a "double bogey", and so on.

# 51

**Currently, there are four tournaments that make up the "Grand Slam" of golf, and the Masters at Augusta is one of them.**

These tournaments are considered the most prestigious in the world of golf and are sought after by the best golfers in the world to win the title.

The Masters at Augusta is one of the most important tournaments and is held at the Augusta National Golf Club in Georgia, United States.

The tournament takes place during the first full week of April every year and attracts the best golfers in the world.

The US Open is another Grand Slam tournament and is organized by the United States Golf Association (USGA).

It is held annually at various golf courses in the United States in June.

The Open Championship, also known as the British Open, is the oldest golf tournament in the world and is held annually at a golf course in the United Kingdom.

It is organized by the Royal and Ancient Golf Club of St. Andrews and takes place in July.

Finally, the PGA Championship is organized by the Professional Golfers' Association of America (PGA) and is held at various golf courses in the United States in May.

Winning all four Grand Slam tournaments is considered one of the greatest achievements in a golfer's career, and only five players have accomplished it in the history of golf: Gene Sarazen, Ben Hogan, Gary Player, Jack Nicklaus, and Tiger Woods.

# 52

## Why does golf pay so much?

Professionals can earn some money in local or
regional tournaments in which they play.

However, golfers earn most of their income from regular checks,
often supplemented by lesson fees and golf shop income.

Furthermore, golf is a sport with a large fan base and followers
worldwide, making it a very popular sport in terms
of marketing and advertising.

Golf event sponsors are often large brands that pay a lot of
money to have their logos and advertisements on golf courses,
on television, and in other media.

Another factor that contributes to high earnings in golf is that
players typically have very long careers compared to other
sports, giving them more time to earn money
and build their professional careers.

Additionally, golf is a global sport, which means that players
have the opportunity to compete and earn money worldwide.

Finally, the large cash prizes awarded in major golf tournaments
such as the Masters, US Open, Open Championship, and PGA
Championship, significantly contribute to high earnings in golf.

These prizes can reach millions of dollars, which attracts the
best players in the world and generates great interest
from the public and sponsors.

# 53

## What is prohibited in golf?

- Asking for advice from anyone other than your partner.

- Marking the line of play when the ball is on the green or while taking a shot.

- Using any artificial device unless it is expressly authorized.

- Carrying more than 14 golf clubs.

- Moving the ball in play, except in specific situations and allowed by the rules of the game.

- Touching the golf course obstacle, such as sand traps, with hands or any tool other than a golf club.

- Touching the ball with the hand, except in very specific situations allowed by the rules of the game.

- Kicking or moving the ball with the feet.

- Intentionally making noise to distract other players during their swing.

- Using any type of performance-enhancing drugs.

- Playing more than one ball at the same time, unless specifically allowed by the course or the rules of the game.

- Using a broken or damaged club during play.

- Throwing or abandoning a golf club during play, unless specifically allowed by the rules of the game.

- Playing out of turn, i.e., hitting the ball before it is the player's turn.

There are many other rules and regulations that govern the game of golf, and players should familiarize themselves with them before participating in the sport.

# 54

## What not to do in golf?

The first basic rule is not to talk or make noise or
gestures that may distract the opponent
while they are hitting the ball.

When a player is going to hit the ball, they must
make sure that the hole is clear or that the group
in front of them is at a safe distance
to avoid hitting them.

Another thing that should not be done in golf is to
walk on the practice fields or on the green with
metal spikes on shoes, as these can
damage the playing surface.

It is also prohibited to remove or damage plants,
trees, or any other natural element
of the golf course.

Players should stay away from hazards such as
ponds, bunkers, and areas with tall grass.

In addition, players should respect etiquette rules
on the golf course, such as not running
on the playing field, not talking loudly,
and avoiding delaying the game.

# 55

**In general, a beginner will need a set of clubs that includes a driver, woods, hybrids, irons, wedges, and a putter.**

In total, it would be 14 clubs allowed by the rules of golf.

To start, a beginner's set of clubs is recommended, which includes a driver, a 3-wood, 3 and 4 hybrids, 5 to 9 irons, pitching wedge, and putter.

This will allow the player to have a variety of clubs for different situations and distances.

However, the most important thing is that the clubs fit the player's needs and abilities.

A beginner may have trouble with long irons and prefer to use more woods or hybrids, for example.

Therefore, it is advisable to seek professional advice to choose the right clubs.

# 56

### What shoes are worn in golf?

To keep your feet dry on the golf course, it is best to choose a waterproof or water-resistant golf shoe.

There are models of waterproof or water-resistant golf shoes that come with a one-year warranty.

Keeping your feet dry is essential to enjoying your time on the course.

In addition, golf shoes should be comfortable and provide good grip on the terrain.

Most golf shoes have soles with cleats that help provide traction on the grass.

They should also be flexible to allow for free foot movement and good breathability.

As for design, golf shoes can vary from classic lace-up models to more modern designs with Velcro closure or no laces at all.

It is important to choose a model that fits well and provides good support, as golfers spend several hours walking on the course.

Finally, golf shoes can also vary in ankle height.

Some models have a low cut that allows for greater freedom of movement, while others have a high cut that provides greater stability and ankle support.

The choice will depend on each player's individual taste and needs.

# 57

## Who is the best female golf player?

American Paige Spiranac was named by Maxim magazine as "The World's Sexiest Woman," being included in the publication's Hot 100 list and chosen for the cover.

The 29-year-old athlete has more than 3 million followers on Instagram.

Paige Spiranac is a well-known personality in women's golf, but it is important to mention that her popularity is mainly due to her physical attractiveness and social media presence rather than her athletic achievements.

As for the best female golf players in terms of results and titles, names such as Annika Sorenstam, Lorena Ochoa, Mickey Wright, Karrie Webb, Patty Berg, among others, stand out.

Each of these players has achieved important victories in high-level tournaments and has left their mark on the history of women's golf.

# 58

**Which hand wears a glove in golf?**

For almost all professional golfers, one glove is enough and it is worn on the hand that is above the hand that grips the club.

This upper hand is responsible for maintaining the grip on the club.

For right-handed golfers, it is the left hand.

For left-handed golfers, the glove is worn on the right hand.

# 59

**What does the letter A mean on a golf club?**

It means "address" and refers to the position
that the player takes when preparing
to hit the golf ball.

It signifies the "alignment" for
executing the shot.

What does the letter E mean in golf?

This refers to the score achieved when the ball
is holed with two strokes less
than the hole's par.

What does the W mean on golf clubs?

This term is the generic name given to clubs
used in the short game.

These include the pitching wedge, lob wedge,
and sand wedge.

They are characterized by their short length
and highly open clubface.

# 60

**A golfer's notebook typically contains a Yardage Book.**

These books contain information on distances, hazards, and the complex greens of each hole on the golf course.

The Yardage Book provides a bit more information than the average scorecard.

# 61

## Skills necessary for golf.

**-Sustained concentration:** maintaining focus on the present moment (shot by shot) and disconnecting from thoughts about the score.

**-Motivation:** knowing what we want, when we want it, and why, having an intention, a plan, and a goal that is interesting and has a reasonable level of demand.

**-Patience:** golf is a sport where results are not always immediate, and constant practice is required to improve.

**-Technique:** it is a fundamental skill in golf, as it determines the accuracy and quality of the shot. It is important to practice it constantly to achieve good execution.

**-Adaptability:** it is a sport played outdoors and on different courses with varying characteristics, so it is important to be able to adapt to different situations and weather conditions.

**-Strategy:** it is important to know when and how to take certain risks on the course to achieve better results.

**-Emotional control:** golf can be a frustrating sport, especially when things don't go as expected. Therefore, it is important to have good emotional control to maintain concentration and not affect performance on the course.

# 62

**How many degrees does a golf club have?**

The clubface typically has between 9 and 14 degrees of loft or angle of the clubface.

Woods 3 and 5: are used for a shot where either not as much distance as the driver is needed or more precision is required, as well as for long shots from the fairway.

In addition to woods, irons also have different degrees of loft.

Generally, long irons (2-4) have a lower loft (between 18 and 28 degrees) and are used for longer shots, while short irons (9-PW) have a higher loft (between 40 and 48 degrees) and are used for shorter shots and greater precision.

Wedges, on the other hand, can have lofts ranging from 50 to 64 degrees and are used for short shots around the green.

The putter, finally, does not have as pronounced of a loft and usually has between 2 and 5 degrees.

It is important to note that the variety of lofts and degrees of the clubs allows golfers to adjust their game to different situations on the course.

# 63

**In golf, the term "fat shot" refers to a stroke in which the clubhead hits the ground before making contact with the ball.**

This type of shot can be caused by a variety of factors, such as poor ball contact, bad posture, faulty swing technique, or simply by choosing the wrong club for the situation.

When a player hits a fat shot, the speed of the clubhead is significantly reduced before making contact with the ball, which can result in reduced distance and a lower, less controlled ball flight.

Players may also feel an uncomfortable vibration in their hands and arms after a heavy shot.

To avoid hitting a fat shot, it's important to maintain proper posture, position the ball correctly for the club, and ensure that the swing is executed correctly.

Players can also benefit from practicing hitting from different surfaces, such as rough or sand, to improve their technique and avoid heavy shots.

In general, hitting a fat shot is considered a mistake in golf, and players often work hard to avoid this type of shot in their game.

# 64

**"Fore" is an expression commonly used in golf to warn other players on the golf course that a golf ball has been struck and may be headed their way.**

The word "Fore" comes from the military term "fore-caddy," which was used on Scottish golf courses in the 18th century to describe the person in charge of finding lost golf balls.

Over time, the expression "Fore" became a common warning in golf.

Golf players often shout "Fore" after hitting a ball that may be headed towards other players, spectators, or employees on the golf course.

This can happen, for example, when a ball is hit off the fairway and heading towards a group of players on another hole or towards the practice area.

It is important for golf players to be alert to "Fore" shouts and take measures to avoid being hit by a flying golf ball.

This may include ducking, covering with arms, or quickly moving away from the area.

Overall, the shout of "Fore" is an important component of etiquette and safety in golf, and players are expected to use it responsibly and effectively to prevent accidents.

# 65

**Cleaning golf clubs is an important part of equipment maintenance and can improve their performance and durability.**

Steps to clean golf clubs:

- **Equipment preparation:** Before starting to clean the clubs, it's important to have all the materials at hand. You'll need a bucket or large container, warm water, mild soap (such as liquid dish soap), a soft toothbrush, and a clean, dry cloth.

- **Soak the clubs:** Fill the bucket with warm water and a small amount of mild soap. Make sure the water doesn't reach the shaft of the club. Submerge the club head in the water and let it soak for a few minutes. This will help loosen embedded dirt and mud.

- **Gentle brushing:** After soaking the clubs, use a soft toothbrush to gently scrub the club head and remove dirt. Be sure to pay attention to the grooves on the club head, which can accumulate dirt and debris. Avoid scrubbing too hard or using a brush that's too hard, as this can scratch or damage the club surface.

- **Rinse and dry:** Once you've finished brushing the clubs, rinse them with clean water to remove any soap residue. Then, dry the club head with a clean, dry cloth. Be sure to thoroughly dry the clubs before storing them in the golf bag.

Additionally, some golfers also use special golf club cleaning wipes or specific cleaning products to help remove dirt and debris from golf clubs.

But basic cleaning with warm water and mild soap is enough to keep the clubs clean and in good working condition.

# 66

## What golf club hits the farthest?

There are 9 different types of iron clubs.

Irons 1, 2, 3, and 4 are used for distances up to 190 meters and are the most difficult to use.

Irons 6, 7, and 8 reach up to 140 meters, and iron 9 is used for distances up to 110 meters.

In general, the golf club that can hit the farthest is the driver, also known as wood 1.

This club is designed to hit the golf ball with the maximum possible distance and is used at the tee box.

The driver has a large and round head, which allows it to provide a large amount of energy to the golf ball at the moment of impact.

In addition, the driver has a long and flexible shaft that helps players generate speed and power in the swing.

However, the distance that can be achieved with the driver depends on several factors, such as the player's skill and technique, wind conditions, the type of golf ball, and the golf course's surface.

Regarding iron clubs, each one is designed for a specific distance.

The lower irons, from 1 to 4, are designed for longer distances and are more challenging to use due to their lower loft angle.

The middle irons, from 5 to 7, are easier to control and are designed for medium distances.

The upper irons, from 8 to 9, are the easiest to use and are used for shorter distances and approaches to the green.

# 67

**The green jacket in golf is the prize awarded to the winner of the Masters tournament at Augusta, one of the four major professional golf tournaments.**

The tournament is held annually at Augusta National Golf Club in Georgia, USA.

The tradition of awarding a green jacket to the winner of the Masters tournament began in 1949.

At that time, members of the Augusta National Golf Club began wearing green jackets as a uniform to distinguish themselves from visitors during the tournament.

A year later, it was decided that the tournament winners should also receive a green jacket as a prize.

The green jacket quickly became a symbol of distinction and prestige in the world of golf.

Only the champions of the Masters tournament can wear the green jacket on the golf course throughout the year following their victory.

In addition, the winner must return the jacket to the club at the end of their year as champion to be kept in the winners' locker room.

The green jacket has been awarded to many of the world's top golfers, including Jack Nicklaus, Tiger Woods, Phil Mickelson, and Jordan Spieth, among others.

It is one of the most prestigious and coveted prizes in the world of golf and represents the most significant achievement in the career of a professional golfer.

# 68

**The timing for changing golf clubs depends on several factors, such as frequency of use, care and maintenance given, and the player's level of play.**

Below are some indicators that may signal the time to change golf clubs:

**–Wear on the grip:** golf club grips are an essential part of the equipment, as they provide the necessary grip and stability for playing. If the grip is worn or has become slippery, it may need to be replaced. Generally, golf club manufacturers recommend changing grips after 40 rounds or every 1-2 years of regular use.

**–Wear on the clubhead:** the golf clubhead can wear down over time due to impacts and natural wear and tear. If the clubhead is worn, deformed, or damaged, it can affect the performance of the club and may need to be replaced.

**–Change in skill level:** if a golf player experiences a significant improvement in their skill level, they may need to consider changing their golf clubs. A more advanced player may require clubs with specific features, such as greater distance or precision, that are not found in basic level golf clubs.

**–Change in game needs:** a golfer's needs can change over time. For example, if a player is recovering from an injury or has changed their playing style, they may require different golf clubs to meet their needs.

**–Usage time:** as golf clubs age, they may lose their performance capabilities, especially if they are not given the proper care and maintenance. If golf clubs have been regularly used for several years, they may need to be replaced to improve performance.

# 69

## What do the colors of the flags in golf mean?

The flag is the ultimate symbol of the hole, indicating to the player its location and target.

There are flags of different types, colors, and even designs, carrying indications about the position of the flag within the Green, informing the player whether it is short (red), medium (blue), or long (white).

In addition to the red, blue, and white colors that indicate the position of the flag on the green, there are also other color combinations used in golf.

For example, a yellow flag may indicate a cautionary situation on the course, such as a water hazard or a construction area.

On the other hand, some competitions or tournaments may use special flags to indicate certain situations.

For instance, a black flag may indicate disqualification in the event of a serious breach of the rules of golf, while a green flag may indicate that play is allowed on the green after a temporary suspension due to a storm or inclement weather.

Overall, the color of the flag in golf serves as a visual guide for players to know the position of the flag and the distance from which the hole is located, enabling them to adjust their shots and plan their playing strategy.

# 70

## What happens if a golf ball hits you?

If a player's moving ball accidentally hits anyone, including the player or any external influence, there is no penalty for any player, even if the ball hits the opponent or any of their caddies or equipment.

However, if the player intentionally hits someone with their ball, they could be disqualified from the tournament and face more severe consequences.

# 71

**The most expensive golf club in the world is the Long Nosed Putter, which bears the stamp of Andrew Dickson and dates back to the year 1700.**

This club is considered the most valuable in the world due to its rarity, authenticity, and the history behind its creation.

The most notable feature of the Long Nosed Putter is its length, measuring around 90 centimeters.

In addition, its design resembles that of a hockey stick, with a flat and wide tip instead of a traditional golf club head.

The club was sold at auction in 2017 for the astonishing amount of $181,000.

This record-breaking figure was reached due to the authenticity of the club, which had been verified by experts in the field.

It is said that the Long Nosed Putter was originally used by a Scottish golfer named Andrew Dickson, who was a prominent golf club maker in the 1700s.

It is believed that only a few examples of this club were ever made, making it a true rarity in the world of golf.

# 72

**Golf balls have dimples to improve their aerodynamics
in the air and their ability to travel farther.**

When a golf ball moves through the air, the air moves around
the ball, which creates an area of pressure behind
it that acts to slow it down.

This effect is known as "drag" or "air resistance".

The dimple design on the surface of the golf ball helps to reduce
this drag effect by creating a turbulent layer of air around the
ball, which reduces the area of pressure behind it.

In other words, the dimples make the ball travel farther
by decreasing air resistance.

As a golf ball moves through the air, the dimples create small
whirlpools in the air that help to stabilize its movement.

These whirlpools also decrease air resistance
and increase the speed of the ball.

The number and shape of the dimples on a golf ball can vary,
which affects its ability to travel farther.

Modern golf balls typically have between 300 and 500 dimples,
which are arranged in specific patterns on the surface of the ball.

These patterns can be circular, hexagonal,
or X-shaped, for example.

# 73

**The maximum weight of a golf ball is established by the rules of The Royal and Ancient Golf Club of St Andrews and the United States Golf Association.**

According to these rules, the maximum weight allowed for a golf ball is 45.93 grams.

In addition to weight, the rules also establish a minimum diameter of 42.67 millimeters and a maximum velocity of 76 meters per second (or 250 feet per second) for golf balls used in official competitions.

The weight limit for golf balls was established to prevent players from using heavier balls to gain an unfair advantage in terms of distance and control.

The maximum allowed velocity was also established to ensure that golf balls do not move at speeds that could jeopardize the safety of players or spectators.

It is important to note that although these rules establish the maximum limits for the weight, diameter, and velocity of golf balls, ball manufacturers typically produce balls that conform to these standards to ensure that they are legal for use in official competitions.

# 74

**Tiger Woods is one of the most successful and recognized golfers of all time, and he has earned a tremendous amount of money throughout his professional career.**

According to reports, Tiger Woods has earned over $120 million in tournament prize money alone throughout his career.

In addition to these winnings, Woods has generated a great deal of income from sponsorships and commercial deals with well-known brands such as Nike, Rolex, American Express, and Gillette, among others.

Forbes estimates Tiger Woods' net worth to be around $800 million, making him one of the wealthiest athletes in the world.

Throughout his career, he has been a leader in sponsorship earnings and has set a number of financial records, including being the first athlete to earn over $1 billion in sponsorship and commercial deals alone.

Additionally, Woods has been a successful entrepreneur, with investments in a variety of businesses and projects.

He has also been generous with his money, donating millions of dollars to charitable organizations and establishing his own foundation, the Tiger Woods Foundation, which focuses on providing access to education and health for young people.

# 75

**Tiger Woods achieved his first hole-in-one at the age of 8 in the presence of his father, Earl Woods.**

This early accomplishment was a sign of the outstanding ability Tiger would have in the sport of golf and was the beginning of a legendary career.

As for sponsorships, Nike has been a key sponsor for Tiger Woods throughout his career.

The company signed him in 1996 and has since been a constant presence in Tiger's life.

In fact, after the extramarital scandals that affected Tiger's career in 2009, Nike was the only major brand that stood firm and continued to support him.

Despite the numerous sponsorships Tiger Woods has had throughout his career, Nike has been a significant brand in the golfer's life.

In addition to apparel and equipment, Tiger has had his own line of Nike products that has generated significant revenue.

The Nike brand has been associated with Tiger Woods' image and personality in the world of golf and has been an integral part of his success on the course and in the business world.

# 76

**Phil Mickelson, one of the greatest golfers in history and a former world number one, lost more than $40 million in casino games between 2010 and 2014, according to his biographer in a book.**

However, during those years of losses in gambling, Mickelson was earning $40 million per season.

Currently, the golfer has a net worth of over $400 million, making him the third richest American player after Tiger Woods and Michael Jordan.

His record of professional titles includes 51 wins, including 6 Majors: 3 Masters Tournament, 2 PGA Championships, and 1 Open Championship.

# 77

## Who is the best golfer of all time?

It is a highly debated topic among golf fans and experts.

Jack Nicklaus is considered by many to be the greatest of all time due to his impressive achievements in his career.

He won 18 major championships (Masters Tournament, U.S. Open, The Open Championship, and PGA Championship), a record that has yet to be surpassed.

Nicklaus also won 73 PGA Tour events and was one of the most consistent golfers of his time.

His ability to remain competitive for decades and on different courses makes him one of the most successful golfers in history.

However, other golfers have also left a significant mark on the sport, such as Tiger Woods, who has won 15 major championships and 82 PGA Tour events, records that put him in the conversation for the greatest golfer of all time.

Other golfers such as Arnold Palmer, Bobby Jones, and Ben Hogan have also been considered some of the best in the history of the sport.

# 78

**Golf is a very popular sport around the world, and the numbers reflect the popularity of golf in the United States, Japan, and China.**

In the United States, golf is one of the most popular sports, and there are a large number of golf courses throughout the country.

In fact, according to the National Golf Association, there are around 18,000 golf courses in the United States and approximately 26 million golfers in the country.

In Japan, golf is also very popular and has long been considered an elite sport.

Despite having a smaller population than the United States, there are around 2,500 golf courses in Japan and approximately 13 million golfers.

In China, golf has become increasingly popular in recent years, especially among the growing middle class in the country.

Although golf was only introduced to China a few decades ago, there are already around 600 golf courses and approximately 5 million golfers in the country.

It is important to note that the numbers may vary depending on the source and that the popularity of golf in different countries can also be affected by cultural and economic factors.

However, these numbers provide a general idea of the reach of golf in different parts of the world.

# 79

## What type of grass is used on golf courses?

There are several types of grasses used on golf courses, and the choice of grass type will depend on various factors such as climate, geographic location of the golf course, amount of sunlight it receives, and amount of traffic it receives.

One of the most common types of grass used on golf courses is Bermuda grass, which you mention in your question.

Bermuda grass is known for its strong root system and its ability to grow in clusters.

This makes it an excellent choice for greens and fairways, as it can be cut very low to achieve a smooth and uniform surface.

Another type of grass commonly used on golf courses is Bent grass, which is softer and more tolerant of cutting than Bermuda grass.

Bent grass is popular on golf courses in colder climates, as it can withstand cold temperatures and frost.

Other types of grasses used on golf courses include Ryegrass, which is commonly used in the cooler regions of the world, and Zoysia grass, which is popular on golf courses in warm and humid climates.

# 80

**Regarding the area, an 18-hole golf course requires 57 to 73 hectares of usable land.**

If you have trouble visualizing hectares, it's worth noting that one hectare is equivalent to 10,000 square meters; comparisons to golf courses can be somewhat imprecise.

In addition to the surface area of the golf course itself, additional areas are needed for parking, practice facilities, clubhouse, etc.

Depending on the location and design of the golf course, more or less land may be required.

For example, a golf course in a mountainous area may require more land to accommodate elevations and slopes.

It's worth noting that while the total surface area of the golf course may vary, the most important thing is the quality of the design and maintenance to ensure a good playing experience for golfers.

# 81

## How many golf courses are there?

As of the end of 2016, there were 33,161 golf courses spread across 208 of the world's 245 countries, representing an 85% global diffusion rate of the sport.

It's important to note that the number of golf courses in the world may vary over time, as golf courses may open and close for various reasons, such as local economy, changes in demand, changes in laws and regulations, etc.

In addition, while golf is popular in many countries around the world, its popularity varies by region.

For example, while golf is very popular in countries like the United States, Scotland, and Japan, it is less common in other countries.

# 82

**A golfer should consume about 50% of their diet in carbohydrates, including whole grain cereals such as oats, brown rice, wheat or potatoes and sweet potatoes.**

In addition, fruits and vegetables should
not be overlooked.

Carbohydrates are the body's preferred source of energy.

They also need protein for building and
repairing muscle tissue.

Proteins can be found in foods such as lean meats,
fish, eggs, low-fat dairy, and legumes.

Omega-3 fatty acids, found in salmon, mackerel, and tuna,
are important for cardiovascular health
and cognitive performance.

As for beverages, golfers need to stay hydrated during the
game, so it's important to consume water and sports
drinks with electrolytes to replenish nutrients
lost through sweating.

During tournaments, golfers often have a team of
nutritionists and chefs who prepare balanced and healthy
meals for them, tailored to their specific needs
and game schedule.

# 83

## How much does a golf course cost?

Building a golf course in Mexico on 65 hectares, which is equivalent to 120 soccer fields, costs between 6 and 8 million dollars depending on earth movement and design type, according to Pizá.

These expenses can increase up to 20 million dollars.

Just the green alone represents an expense of 50,000 dollars.

The construction cost includes land preparation, construction of greens, sand traps, water hazards, grass seeding, irrigation installation, and building facilities such as the clubhouse, driving range, and locker rooms.

In addition, after construction, the maintenance costs of the golf course can be very high as the quality of the grass, irrigation, maintenance of facilities, among other things, must be maintained.

# 84

## What are the names of golf shots?

**–Putt:** it is the stroke that finishes the hole, and it is given from the green, where precision is essential. Using the putter, we make a stroke without flight, in which the ball rolls into the hole.

**–Approach:** it must be precise and have enough power to reach the green, but not too much to overshoot it. Its quality can have a significant impact on the final result of a hole, as it allows players to reduce their number of putts and improve their chances of making birdie or par.

**–Drive:** it is the initial stroke and is given from the tee, where the goal is to cover the maximum distance possible and leave the ball in a good position for the next stroke.

**–Iron:** it is a stroke with an iron club that is used on the fairway or in the rough. The aim is to control the distance and direction of the ball.

**–Chip:** it is a short stroke that is made from the rough or near the green, with the aim of getting the ball as close to the hole as possible.

**–Bunker shot:** it is used when the ball has landed in a sand bunker. It is made with a special club called a wedge and consists of getting the ball out of the bunker and onto the green or as close to the hole as possible.

**–Flop shot:** it is a high-precision stroke used to overcome obstacles such as trees or bunkers and get the ball as close to the hole as possible.

**–Punch shot:** it is a stroke used to get out of difficult situations such as trees or strong winds. It is made with a low iron club, and the aim is to keep the ball low and move it towards the target.

**–Pitch:** it is a short to medium distance shot made near the green, with the aim of making the ball roll into the hole. It is used when the ball is farther from the green than in the chip but still close enough not to require a full stroke.

**–Fairway:** it is the stroke made in the fairway area, which is the short and uniform terrain between the tee and the green. It is used to advance the ball towards the green with precision.

# 85

## How many liters of water does a golf course consume?

The sustainability of these facilities has always been questioned due to the abundant water they require for maintenance.

On average, water consumption for a golf course is estimated to range between 200,000 and 300,000 m3 per year.

It is important to note that water consumption can vary significantly depending on several factors such as the climate and region where the golf course is located, the type of grass used, the frequency and amount of irrigation, and the water conservation measures implemented.

Typically, golf courses use sophisticated and advanced irrigation systems to optimize water consumption and reduce their environmental impact.

In addition, many facilities are also implementing sustainable practices such as capturing and reusing rainwater and utilizing technologies that allow for precise measurement and control of water consumption on the golf course.

# 86

**The record of 27 strokes in the first nine holes set by Jim Furyk at the 2013 BMW Championship is considered one of the greatest achievements in professional golf history.**

Furyk achieved this score at the Conway Farms Golf Club in Lake Forest, Illinois, an 18-hole golf course that has hosted several major PGA Tour tournaments.

Furyk is known for being an exceptional player, and his record of 27 strokes in the first nine holes clearly demonstrates this.

Corey Pavin, on the other hand, achieved 26 strokes in the first nine holes of the US Bank Championship in Milwaukee in 2006, which is also considered a great achievement in professional golf history.

# 87

**As for the best score by a player in a golf tournament, the world record for a 72-hole tournament is 254 strokes, which was achieved by Kim Jong-Il, the North Korean leader, in 1994.**

However, this record is not officially recognized by golf's governing bodies due to the special circumstances under which it supposedly took place.

Regarding the records recognized by golf's governing bodies, the best score in a golf tournament is 58 strokes, established by Jim Furyk at the 2016 Travelers Championship at TPC River Highlands in Cromwell, Connecticut.

This record refers to the best score in an 18-hole tournament.

It should be noted that, although these records are impressive, it is more common for players to have much higher scores, as golf is a sport that is very demanding in terms of technique, precision, and strategy.

# 88

**The Royal County Down Golf Club, located in Newcastle, Northern Ireland, is considered by many experts to be one of the best golf courses in the world.**

It was founded in 1889 and designed by Old Tom Morris, one of the pioneers of golf and a legend in the sport.

The course is located in a spectacular setting, with views of the Mourne Mountains and Dundrum Bay, and features a variety of challenging holes that have attracted players from all over the world.

The course has been remodeled several times over the years, and currently is home to two golf courses: the Championship Links course, which is considered one of the best golf courses in the world, and the Annesley Links course, which is a shorter and more accessible course for beginner players.

The Championship Links course has hosted several major championships, including the 2015 Irish Open, and has been praised for its natural beauty and technical challenge.

# 89

**The lowest handicap in golf is not 0, but it can even be negative.**

The handicap is calculated based on the players' results in different matches, and is used to equalize the chances of players at different levels.

For example, a player with a handicap of 0 is considered capable of playing a golf course in the expected number of strokes or par.

A player with a negative handicap has an average of strokes below par, which means they have an exceptionally high level of play.

Professional players often have negative handicaps, some of them even less than -10.

In general, the lower the handicap, the higher the player's level of skill.

# 90

**To achieve playing bogey on each hole and getting some pars, it's important to follow some guidelines:**

**-Practice the swing:** consistency in the swing is key to good results. It's important to dedicate time to practicing this movement and finding the appropriate technique for each player.

**-Know the course:** it's essential to know the course where you will play, know the distance to the obstacles, the location of the holes, and the characteristics of the terrain.

**-Use the appropriate club:** learning to choose the appropriate club for each stroke, according to the distance and type of terrain, can help avoid mistakes and improve the final result.

**-Control the speed of the putt:** putting is one of the most important strokes in golf. To improve, it's necessary to work on precision in the stroke and the speed with which the ball is launched to ensure it reaches the hole.

**-Maintain composure:** golf is a sport that requires a lot of concentration and patience. Maintaining composure in the face of mistakes and difficulties is key to being able to recover and continue playing well.

By following these guidelines and with a lot of practice, it's possible to achieve scoring under 90 strokes in golf.

# 91

## Who goes first in golf?

In informal golf matches, a rotation is generally followed in which each player takes turns going first on the tee box.

This rotation can be established beforehand or decided randomly before the match begins.

In some cases, the player with the lowest handicap may have the honor of going first on the tee box.

In official golf competitions, the player who goes first on the tee box is the one who has been designated as the "lead-off player" for that particular hole.

Generally, the lead-off player in a competition is determined by the result of the previous round or by a draw before the start of the tournament.

In major championships, such as the Grand Slam tournaments, the player with the best world ranking often has the honor of going first.

# 92

Ted Scott, the former caddie who helped Bubba Watson win two green jackets in 2012 and 2014, and most recently caddie for Scottie Scheffler, is very clear that Scheffler has the perfect family environment to keep him grounded and remain the same person despite his success.

Ted shared a funny anecdote about Scheffler and his wife, a conversation they had a week before the Masters, after Scheffler became the world number one following his Match Play win.

"Scheffler told me, 'buddy, my wife asked me to take out the trash.' And I said to her, 'honey, I'm number one.' She said, 'I don't care, go take out the trash!' So, I still have to do my chores."

According to Ted, Scheffler's wife Meredith and his parents, Scott and Diane, have been instrumental in helping him stay grounded and keep his head out of the clouds.

# 93

**John Daly.**

"I've played many times hungover and even once drank on the course."

Until now, Wild Thing was known for his sour demeanor on the golf course, but history will remember his immense anger during the 2015 PGA Championship when he threw his club into the water after signing a 10 on one of his holes.

Now we also know that he has played in PGA tournaments while hungover and has even consumed alcohol during rounds.

These confessions are part of a documentary being prepared by ESPN about the trajectory of the singular American athlete, who can appear in a Stars and Stripes suit at a formal dinner or destroy balls with the speed he imparts on his shots.

"As far as I can remember, my experiences with alcohol have never directly accompanied me on the course...except for one time. It was at a Los Angeles Open. I was playing pretty badly, two or three over par on my first nine holes, so I went for it. What could go wrong? I went into the locker room and drank about five beers in one go. If my memory serves me well, in the last nine holes, I shot four under par. It's the only time I've ever drank during a round, and frankly, I played very well. It helped me that week," Daly confessed.

But his anecdotes with alcohol don't end there: "I wouldn't be able to count the number of times I've stepped onto a course and played while hungover. In fact, there were times when I played in championships while still drunk from being out until five in the morning the night before."

# 94

**Raymond Floyd.**

"They call it golf because all the other four-
letter words were taken."

This always gets a laugh on the course
because we are not immune to a four-letter
word (Fuck) every now and then...
Shit or Damn are usually the most
expressed in Spanish.

Cursing is not something golfers are proud
of, nor is it very classy, but it happens quite
frequently on the golf course.

Ray Floyd pointed this out and essentially let
everyone know that golfers may not be as
refined as most people think, especially
a few decades ago.

# 95

**Chi Chi Rodríguez.**

"Golf is the most fun you can have without taking your clothes off."

Known for his colorful personality, only Chi Chi Rodríguez could get away with such a tempting statement.

You probably know the numerous videos in which Chi Chi brandishes his putter like a fencing saber after sinking a long putt.

This great quote never gets old.

# 96

**Harry Vardon.**

"Don't play too much golf. Two rounds a day are plenty."

The golden age of golf knew how to have a laugh or two.

Unknowingly, Vardon created one of the first "golf memes".

You may have heard a variation of this from your grandpa or boss, and it still holds true today.

# 97

**Ben Hogan.**

"The most important shot in golf
is the next one."

This quote withstands the test of time and is
just as relevant in real-life scenarios.

It is definitely a phrase to keep in mind if you
play in any tournament.

The time commitment for a round of golf
means that you will hit some
pretty bad shots.

If you play golf in a two or four-day
tournament, those mistakes will
start to add up.

The key to anyone's golf game is limiting the
number of bad shots you hit; you can only
do that by looking to the next shot.

# 98

**Bobby Jones.**

"The golf swing is a game that is played
on a five-inch course: the distance
between your ears."

This is one of the most famous golf quotes of
all time, and you've probably seen it displayed
on a lot of golf merchandise in most golf
shops around the world.

It perfectly sums up the game and points
out what elite golfers already know.

The previous generation tended to focus their
efforts on the things they could control:
their mindset.

They almost never talked about technology,
equipment, course conditions, schedules,
and money as much as they do today.

# 99

**Dr. Bob Rotella.**

"Golf is about how well you accept, respond, and score with your mistakes much more than it is a game of your perfect shots."

Dr. Bob is widely known in the world of golf, especially among the professionals of the major tours.

He has worked with the best players in the game for over three decades.

# 100

**Arnold Palmer.**

"Success in this game depends less on the strength of the body than on the strength of the mind and character."

Arnold Palmer was one of the most dominant golfers of the late 1950s and early 1960s, winning seven major titles over seven seasons.

Many golfers don't want to admit that their mental game is what holds them back and keeps their results high.

If Arnold Palmer said that the mental game is so important, we should take it very seriously.

# 101

## Jack William Nicklaus.

"Ninety-nine percent of today's golf balls are better than the players who use them."

Born in Columbus, Ohio on January 21, 1940, he is a retired American golfer, widely regarded as the greatest golfer of all time for having won the most major professional tournaments, a total of 18, and 20 if you count the two U.S. Amateur Opens he won in 1959 and 1961.

His burly appearance and golden hair have earned him the nickname "Golden Bear."

If you have enjoyed the golf curiosities presented in this book, we would like to ask you to share a review on Amazon.

Your opinion is very valuable to us and to other golf lovers who are looking to be entertained and learn new knowledge about this sport.

We understand that leaving a comment can be a tedious process, but we ask that you take a few minutes of your time to share your thoughts and opinions with us.

Your support is very important to us and helps us to continue creating quality content for lovers of this incredible sport.

We appreciate your support and hope that you have enjoyed reading our book as much as we enjoyed writing it.

Thank you for sharing your experience with us!

★ ★ ★ ★ ★

Printed in Great Britain
by Amazon